*it'll make
you think
and touch your heart*

*an escaped bird
an innocent laugh
a poem is a piece of art*

journey ...

a collection of original poems and lyrics

by

Charlie Windermere

Table of Contents

left behind	11
addicted to you	12
due	14
my poems rhyme	17
she waits	18
it is possible	20
that feeling	22
another fall	24
letter	26
always love you	29
black & white	30
desire	32
I missed you	34
trust	36
no more wise	38
pretty face	39
stay	40
you and I	42
I love her	44
a long shot	46
I loved you	48
last kiss	50
without you	52
what is the lack	54
impure	57
a moment	58
this way	59
you are mine	65
could have been	71
she is the one	72

a long night	75
lonely night	76
one day	78
you left	81
what was I thinking	82
your anklet	85
about her	86
depends	88
I am afraid	90
I so miss you	92
love stories	94
the move	95
not when I met you	99
together	100
promise	102
sold	105
persistence	107
feminine	108
humanity is choking	109
boys don't cry	110
there is no tomorrow	112
wait	113
the best thing	114
coexist	116
poised	118
purpose	120
don't give up	121
original	122
now	124
why	126
two people	128
the key	130

a poem	132
journey	134
that one friend	136
rituals	138
not a bad guy	140
the bill	142
try	144
I am you	146
live	148
a new day	150

x

left behind

your face
keeps coming
in my mind

you moved ahead
I am
left behind

all those memories
are still fresh
in my head

the regret
of all the words
left unsaid

your
thought
is all I keep

I
just
can't sleep

addicted to you

you are
the journey
you are
the destination

you are
the labour
you are
the vacation

I crave for you
addicted to you
forever thirsty
and wasted

the taste of you
my blurry view
I am cursed
you're gifted

trapped
in your illusion
I am a mortal
you are divine

you are
the poison
I sip like the
finest wine

due

yet another week
has gone by
Friday evening is here

I slowly walk towards home
the night is icy cold
the sky is clear

it's all the same
the snow, the stars
the full moon

it's almost a month
since I first met you
life is going too soon

remember
your arms around me
the hug

the snowflakes
that moment
that snug

I could still sense
your fragrance
on my overcoat

the smile
you gave me
while fixing my tie knot

you promised
you would call
and we could go for a walk

maybe dine
in candlelight
have a little talk

one more beautiful night
without you
you never called

I know
I know I'll see you again
my heart told

yet again
I will sit
around the fireplace
sipping scotch
thinking of you

your lovely hair
your heavenly fragrance
your laugh, your eyes
I know something
amazing is due

my poems rhyme

you can't look
straight
into my eyes

scared!
you'll see
all your lies

too late
no matter
what you do

these are
my last words
to you

you gave me
so much pain
it's enough this time

I am sad, so sad
my poems
will always rhyme

she waits

It's been years
ever since he left her
telling that
he'll be back soon

every single day
she sits on the hilltop
looking over the path
by the sand dune

the noon slowly fades into a
beautiful evening

the pleasant breeze
messes up
her dark brown hair

her teardrops
dry out on her cheeks
he is still not there

she slowly walks
towards her
small house
beside the fields

the grace she carries
tells everyone
that there is no one else
she needs

she is so calm
calm as the water
behind the floodgates

oh! her heart weeps
as she waits, she waits
and she waits

it is possible

things will be different
unfamiliar, scary and new
but it is possible
to live without you

new perspective, new direction
new way of life, new horizon
a changed view
but it is possible
to live without you

It's was amazing
when we met
the charm, the excitement
the playfulness, the attachment
who would let it go?
I am amongst the few
it is possible
to live without you

crossing the paths
was meant to be
what's next is destiny
never expected
but always knew
it is possible
to live without you

that feeling

well, that feeling
when you hit
rock bottom

when you think
this time 'I've got it'
but you were just so dumb

long story short
here is
the gist

don't tell anyone
as it was kind of
an unexpected twist

so the evening
was romantic
night was even better

we were so passionate
as if nothing else
would ever matter

I fell asleep hoping
for a new beginning
when this night is over

I woke up to see a note
under the lamp
on top of the drawer

I felt stupid
'enough'
is what I had

here is what
that
note said

"don't get
me wrong
I had fun"

"we could
never be together
you are the other one"

another fall

weathers
will change
there will be
another fall

the lonesome trees
will remind me
that you won't be there
to give me a call

the leaves
will fall again
the winds will get cold

time will pass by
we will be
weak and old

remember me
whenever you feel
the breeze on your skin

I'll be thinking of you
fighting through my last days
hoping for an impossible win

If I die waiting for you
and my heart asks
'where is she ?'

I'll whisper
with my last breath
'may be she left before me'

letter

I opened a letter
you wrote me
long ago

I tried many times
but my ego
said 'no'

I was angry
you were
gone

I tossed the letter
never answered
your phone

now my old eyes
struggle
to read it all

I wish
I could get up
and give you a call

to see you once
before I go
the impossible desire
of my soul

like that lonely leaf
holding on
to the old tree
in this harsh fall

I look back
and my heart
aches

they say
you live
your mistakes

how silly
was the reason
I let you go

I opened the letter
you wrote me
long ago

a poet's heart

she didn't realize
the damage
she did

the sky went teary
when she killed
the cupid

scattered in pieces
she teared
it apart

the words sob in silence
she broke
a poet's heart

always love you

you left us today
we were together for so long
thanks for keeping it real

the kids, the grandkids
friends and family
everyone is here
for your last ride, your funeral

you are leaving behind
a big happy family
and your sweetheart

I will miss you so much
and will always love you
you did your part

I look around and smile
an amazing little world of ours
we built together

nothing can replace
your lovely family
I wish the place you've gone
is even better

black & white

there is no zeal
there is
no fight

they ask me why
I always write
in black & white

I wish
I could tell them
what you did to me

with my
ruined emotions
it's only darkness I see

remember that
new year's eve
when I waited all night

you never came
oh! the heartache
took my life's light

that long night alone
speaks
the deepest part

when I didn't see you
I left
without my heart

where did you go
you and I
were just so right

I miss you so much
I live and dream
in black & white

desire

I could feel
your breath
on my skin

hesitant
but I gave in
to this sin

your fingers
caressing up
my legs

don't stop
I silently scream
my desire begs

like a red hot knife
have the
butter melt

if only every pore
in my body could tell you
how I felt

I surrender
drowned in
your enclosure

my entire
existence is
oozing pleasure

I missed you

it was snowing last night
and I missed you

the lonely trail
made me think of you

remember our first date?
you were holding my hand
I was walking with you

I miss
every coffee
I had with you

I remember
your innocence
pure as snowflakes

I wish
to relive those moments
whatever it takes

I walk alone
thinking of you

my heart says
across the foggy wall
I will see you

I keep walking
I feel a tug

I am sure you are there
arms open to give me hug

I kept walking
but you were not there

I looked for you
but I didn't see you

it was snowing last night
and I missed you

trust

teardrops falling
from her
deep eyes

the confusion
the misunderstanding
the untold lies

her little heart
loved him
the way he was

everything was so beautiful
so pure
flawless like glass

now it all seems blurry
unclear uncertain
like a dense dark smog

he is trying
to make her feel loved
but those memories are a clog

he want her
he needs her
he knows she deserves it all

he thinks this is temporary
in the season of love
this is just another fall

the pieces of her broken heart
chocked her throat
tears hazed her view

she can't trust again
no matter how many times
he says 'I love you'

no more wise

she only turned once
and looked straight
into my eyes

confused, corrupted, captivated
I was no more
wise

pretty face

while I sat on the couch
she closed the door
and walked towards me

suggestive, seductive, sensual
a foot on the couch
she revealed more than
I expected to see

wild, wicked, willing
behind the pretty face
she took me by surprise

judged a book
by it's cover
I wasn't so wise

while you gossip
romanticize, fantasize
while you so wish and pray

forget about those fifty
she took me through
stunning shades of grey

stay

I wish
I close my eyes
and it's over

when it gets harder
time moves
slower

I sob in silence
choking
my soul's shout

I am giving up
I so want to
tap out

a thin string
is keeping me
stay

loved ones
who stand by me
in every way

I'll keep going
I know
you care

you are the light
in darkness
everywhere

you and I

I see you blooming
with the treasure of love
playful radiant
you look so pearled

you and I
in this beautiful world

stay with me
the best is yet to be

I see it in your eyes
what do you see

from skin to soul
'we' are the goal

I submerge in you
you make me whole

when
you are with me
it all seems fine

perfect it is
I am yours
and you are mine

stay in my arms
cozy and curled

you and I
in this beautiful world

I love her

she
laughs
so freely

my
worries
seem silly

our
lives are
a world apart

I am
all mind
she is all heart

she is
too good
for me

my
real face
she'll never see

in my arms
she is
so fragile

with me
her free soul
appears docile

my heart
said yes
mind told no

I love her
so much
I let her go

a long shot

every morning
I get on the train
I see her on the same spot

calm, composed, collected
holding a book
I think she reads a lot

I look forward
to Wednesdays when
she is usually quite dressed

well, it doesn't matter though
I think she is just amazing
I am so impressed

I like the way
she styled her hair
last Friday

I wish
she does it often
but who am I to say

next time
I'll start a conversation
if I could

I tried once
I was so close
God! She smells good

it may seem
but it is not so easy
it's a long shot, I won't lie

I am different you know
if she is not into girls
let's hope she is at least bi

I loved you

candles are melting
the diner
is empty

I stare at the door
it's you
I want to see

I kept waiting
but you
never came

I loved you
so much
what a shame

servers are whispering
they feel
sad about me

you left me halfway
like a lonely boat
in the sea

I hold
my tears
take a deep sigh

I get up
and leave
thinking why did you lie

I am so hurt
I will live
with this pain

no one
can see my tears
as I walk in the rain

last kiss

there is nothing
I can
forget

a lot more
to live with
I bet

just gone
left
you disappeared

so much trust
this
I never feared

what do
I do now
this is new

I am so sad
so lost
I so miss you

I remember
our last kiss
your face so pretty

your shivering lips
it was snowing
in New York City

without you

the rains
don't rhyme
as before

the waves
no more
kiss the shore

the autumn
breeze doesn't
romance anymore

the maple leaves
has no one
to crackle for

you were present
in every bit
around me

I feel your absence
in everything
I see

you are the life
departing
slowly

without you
even loneliness
is lonely

what is the lack

it's an hour
past midnight
they are closing
the pub

the girl behind the bar
came near me
she said, "It's time to close"
giving my shoulder a tender rub

I look around
the bar is empty
it's only me left there

your fragrance
is always with me
but I see you nowhere

It's an hour past midnight
I see from the glass window
of this tiny bar

it's pouring rain
in this cold December night
where are you? ...... far, so far

I gulp the last sip of scotch
leaving the empty glass
on the table

I hope
I might stop thinking of you
but no, I wasn't able

I leave some money
on the table
and grab my overcoat

one more evening is gone
your smile, your eyes
you, you are the only thought

wrapped
in my overcoat and scarf
I slowly walk
in the rain

your face in candlelight
your innocence
your memories is all I have
pain, so much pain

I live
a day at a time
and a night another

I could not feel my tears
they are one
with the weather

my mind keep asking
I have it all
the things, the stuff
what is the lack?

my heart
weeps stronger
hoping one day
one day you will come back

impure

your curves
make rivers
insecure

I look at you
with attraction pure
thoughts impure

there you are
dressed, done
looking great

here I am
behind you
purposely late

If I could tell you
what I
feel and see

when I follow you
climbing the stairs
in front of me

a moment

today
she is born
she has arrived

how we so grow up
in a moment
when I saw her, I realized

I walked towards her
for the first time
I held my little girl

my tear drop fell
on her cheek
like a pearl

she smiled
just like her mother
I couldn't tell apart

my eyes
gave her a drop
of my melting heart

this way

still waiting
if she is going to walk in
for dinner

its past 20 minutes
my palms are sweating

….I am still waiting

I remember
when I asked you
and you said, "I'll see"

I told you the place
and requested
"do come if you are free"

you just smiled
and
walked away

I took it as a 'Yes'
and thought
you want it this way

its half an hour now
and I don't
see you

I was all prepared
to say it
to you

I've got
the best corner
and the candles are up

the table
the wine
it's all set up

It's nearly an hour now
I don't know
what to say

I am feeling so heavy
may be you really want it
'this way'

I take
a deep breath
and stare at the floor

I so want
to see you
walk in through that door

I loosen my knot
and take
a sip of wine

I close my eyes
and hope
it's all going to be fine

wait !

I hear footsteps
getting closer
from behind

oh! God,
it has to be her
when I turn around and find

fingers crossed
I hold my breath
it's only you in my mind

oh! God,
it has to be her
when I turn around and find

I lean
on the table
and close my eyes

I so want to
hear my name
in your voice

the footsteps stopped
I hear
no noise

It has to be her
I have
no choice

and!

your arms
hugging me
from back

the kiss
you gave me
on my neck

I feel your breath
I feel
your presence

your curly hairs
your
heavenly fragrance

I am sure
it's you.
I turned around

and guess what?
It's you
I found

I looked
into your eyes
smiled and looked away

I always knew
you want it
'this way'

you are mine

snowy dark night
the moon is struggling hard
behind the cloud

I so wish I could see you
my desires
are screaming aloud

wrapped in a warm coat
I slowly walk
towards that lonely lamp post

that's where
the lounge is
there I'll see my host

ever since
I met you here
I come every now and then

the song, the couch
the scotch, the milieu

that moment lives in my soul
saying one day
I will see you again

remember
when I first saw you
I did ask your name

I politely confirmed
if I got it right
you smiled saying, 'Yes that's
the same ..."

It's been so long
I never saw
you again

your eyes, your Smile
only your memory
is remain

every time I think of you
a deep sigh
my heart takes

I know it is far from possible
these are just desire
my heart makes

I reach
the lounge
take my usual spot

my heart
still awaits you
believe it or not

I remember the song
this band was playing
when we met

wine on your lips
your lovely dress
trying to say so much
in few words

you were
so innocent
I could never forget

listening to
the same song today
is such a glee

an even soothing voice
touches my senses
saying, 'excuse me'

I slowly
turned around
and for a moment I froze

those eyes, those curls
that fragrance
'you' were there, so close

I turn back
sip my scotch and tell myself
'It just cannot be'

it can't be happening
something is
certainly wrong with me

you slowly walked in front
leaned a little
and came closer

I could feel my own heart
your fragrance
was getting fresher

you asked me
if I would click
a picture for you

I couldn't say a word
I waited so long
for this moment
moments that are only a few

you don't even
remember me!
off course

but now I know
why I so missed you
you were the reason
the desire, the force

'sure'... I said with a big smile
you were looking the same
so elegant, so innocent
so pretty, so fine

I am never going to
let you disappear again
you are mine, you are mine
you are mine

could have been

they crossed paths
so many times
as moon and sun
they never met

the glittering stars
though beautiful
distracted them
never helped

as the time passed
they both disappeared
not ever
to be seen

unknown, unaware,
unconscious of
what actually
they could have been

she is the one

oh Man, look!
she is sobbing.
she is walking away

won't listen to you
no matter
what you say

she can
hear you
calling her name

you know her
She won't turn
yes, she is the same

you have known her
known her
since long

her favorite flowers
the dress she likes
and she loves that song

you know she loves you
and you love her too
you die for her
yes, yes you do

all days
are not same
these are tough time

this moment
shall pass too, yes
it's going to be fine

hold her
kiss her
don't let her go

she craves
the love
lost long ago

you are the man
keeping strong
when times are tough

you are
the world for her
for her that's enough

you know
times will change
and this is not done

you know
she's the one, she's the one
she is the one

a long night

the sound of
burning wood crackling

the falling snow outside

the unfinished book
beside the blanket

your memories
and the moonlight

it's going to be
a long night

it's going to be
a long night...

lonely night

snowy lonely night
I walk on the streets
of this city

your eyes...
I still remember
they were so pretty

days, months
years
are passing by

every moment
something inside me
asks, "why?"

you are so far
yet
so near

there are
words unsaid
that's the only fear

I remember
every bit of you
that's the beauty

snowy lonely night
I walk on the streets
of this city

one day

its Christmas Eve
snowing
outside

but warm
and nice
in here

I miss you
so much
you are not here

when it started getting dark
the lights
came up

I wouldn't see you
beside the fireplace
I had this fear

I pour
some wine
thinking of you

with every sip
I take a deep breath
I so miss you

remember the first time
you walked in
for dinner

your curly hairs
your heavenly fragrance
nothing is here

I know you
like this red blanket,
you told me once

the sound of the saxophone
that lovely tune
you want to hear

It's getting late
dawn
is here

the glass is empty
I am feeling
the wine

I don't know when I fell asleep
thinking one day
one day you will be mine

you left

I quietly sit
on this old bench
in a calm winter night

it's been so long you left
I should've hugged you
after our last fight

I look
at the moon
through these leaves

I
so miss you
my heart weeps

the silence
the stars
the stillness around me

I am
never alone
your memories surround me

what was I thinking

she left
her coffee
unfinished

I see her lips
marked on
that mug brim

she stormed
out the café
in such fury

this is it!
I could see
things getting blurry

her fragrances
she left behind
is disappearing

I could see her walking away
ah! that lovely dress
she is wearing

I wish she turns back
and gives me that look
as always

and I could make
everything calm
just like those beautiful days

I know
she was upset
and started the fight

but how could
I forget those dinners
and candle light

this is it...!
I can't see 'you'
anymore

that left turn 'you' took
departs my heart
from your

well... this time
it's over
my heart is sinking
oh God...
I ruined it
what was I thinking

I take
a deep breath
and stretch my leg

and there it is
right there
'You' forgot your bag

I stare
at your duffle
and look at your mug

well, well, well
there 'you' are
laughing, waiting for a hug

your anklet

I could see you
in that cocktail dress
I have my eyes on you

the lounge is packed
but I have
a clear view

remember that night?
we had too much
to drink

I never saw you again
waited So long
I am on the brink

I know it's you
it is you!
I can't wait

those curls, those eyes
I so remember
your diamond anklet

about her

the fall leaves
crackle
under my feet

the silence!
I hear my own
heart beat

the lake water
tries to
talk to me

I hear a yell
when I sit
by the sea

pure bliss
havens' kiss
bluest sky
my deepest sigh

amazing she was
her absence
screams louder

can I tell you
more
about her

depends

see
it can go
either way

I ask you out
and depends
what you say

you can
judge me now
on superficial things

go on your way
and accept
what destiny brings

or we can
make an effort
one step a time

get to know more
and find if our
rhythms rhyme

there is
a lot more
that can be

would you like
to dine
with me

I am afraid

with you
the autumn
feels different

the breeze
carries your
mesmerizing scent

your smile
your laugh
your presence

I breathe you
I can't image
a distance

I don't know
If you are
where I am

I am afraid
this feeling makes
me overwhelm

I hope
one day
you will say 'I do'

what a moment
that was
when I met you

I so miss you

every evening
I sit
on this rock

the waves
reach my feet
giving a tender stroke

as the day fades
in lovely colours
of chrome

with every stroke
the sea tells me
to go home

my heart sinks
as the sun
goes down

you left me alone
in this
busy town

if you feel
the pain
in my words

come home
with the
returning birds

come home
for I so, so
miss you

everyday I wait here
wearing
your favourite blue

love stories

the lesser known
love stories
amongst us

a soldier's wife
waiting, worried
alone, anxious

the hug, the kiss
the warmth
you feel everyday

her life is different
it's the price
she has to pay

ask her
how is she?
'I am ok', she'll say

with a smile
on her face
she will downplay

the move

her beauty glows
in candlelight
the pinot gets finer
when she lips the wine

gorgeous, gracious, genuine
pure soul
so sensual
she is divine

when she licks
the wine
off her lips

I struggle
to control
my desire drips

as she gets up
I see her
from head to toe

my morals
are dropping
low, low, low

the rope
I am walking
is getting narrow

her fragrance
her aura
her carelessness

the things I imagine
when I look at her
ah! you curvy goddess

stranger a week ago
she is
trusting me now

I know it's fast
but here we are
somehow

I kept pouring
her more wine
determined

tonight
I'll make
her mine

she is
losing
herself

her
judgement
is going deaf

she came closer
and held
my hand

I gaze in her dusky eyes
It tells me 'something'
I so understand

she is comfortable
she is high
she is so giving in

she is vulnerable
she is craving
she is so blushing

I made
the move
picked her up
and gently put her on the bed

I lean on her
looked right into her eyes
she is ready
her face turned red

I whispered in her ear
 …'sleep tight'
then I kissed her forehead

she pulled me closer
smiled and said
'so, chivalry is not dead'

not when I met you

there is a bit of me
that died today

it's not
when I met you

it's when you disappeared
you took my breath away

together

together
in thick
and in thin

in life
we lose some
some we win

in good times
I'll be with you
to party and cheer

when it's rough
I'll stand by you
together we'll steer

you and I
are
forever

the bridge of life
we'll cross it
together

when everyone leaves
count on me
I will stay

fearless, committed
together
we'll go all the way

promise

let me hold your hand
and follow you
on this journey

as I trust you
and take the first step
anxiously

I promise
you are my everything
my friend, my companion
my family

promise me
you will love me, respect me
as I embark
on this voyage with you

I trust you, believe in you
I am hopeful as I see
the dream, the horizon
the view

we live in times
where I don't need you
for anything but true love

I looked for you, and chose you
as I wondered around
like a lonely dove

I promise to pick you up
if you ever stumble
I will do my part

tell me, tell me
that you've got my back
you'll never let 'us' fall apart

I promise you
I'll be your love, your comfort
your hug, your kiss

promise me you will be
my pride, my strength
my dear, my bliss

I will be
the woman of your home
promise me
you will be the man of my life

I will always love you
I promise you today
as I become
your wife

sold

success, wealth
ambitions, the race
my hustling life

sternness wins
slaying playfulness
the eternal strife

like the first
sprinkle of rain
on an ever waiting desert

your eyes pierced
my clogged soul
and it doesn't hurt

like the spring sprouts
after a long
harsh cold

she smiled once
and
I was sold

*the key
is to know
when to let go*

*when the tide
is against
go with the flow*

persistence

persistent, passionate
she worked
so hard

dream, desire
clear as crystal
no façade

trained, tough
for her enough
was not enough

sweated, suffered
but she
never gave up

hurt, humiliated
her quest
was called lame

incredible, impossible
I saw a moth
kill the flame

feminine

looks fragile
immensely capable
calm, caring, cute

the feminine energy
is irreplaceable
it has no substitute

a mother
a sister, a daughter
a spouse

without a woman
a home
is just a house

when life's tough
'she' gives me a hug
and it all seems fine

mother (nature) knew it all
that's why
half the world is feminine

humanity is choking

would you look at
what is
happening

can you feel
the humanity
is choking

innocent lives
are brutally
murdered

where is it heading
I am scared
to move forward

'an eye for an eye
will leave
us all blind'

let's preserve
whatever humanity
we could find

boys don't cry

I saw
a man
crying today

It felt strange
as boys don't cry
they say

It's
a man's world
he was told

always hiding
his emotions
he grew old

I asked him
why he is hiding
his tears

he whispered
disappointing everyone
is what he fears

crumbling him
under that
'masculine' way

the society
failed him
today

there is no tomorrow

live in the present
there is
no tomorrow

no one knows when
you'll rest in peace
leaving everyone in sorrow

say 'I love you', 'Thank You'
'I am sorry' often
tell your loved ones
how you feel

when the moment comes
there will be no extra time
that you could
beg, borrow, or steal

wait

for some, life is more agonizing
than death

the hatchlings wait for
the dead bird

till their last breath

the best thing

a journey is
to a destination
travelling uselessly
is no fun

scarcity makes
things desirable
out of the million
you want that 'one'

a never-ending book
an endless
movie

you don't want to keep going
something constant
is not groovy

we all have a limited time
childhood, adulthood
and the old age

day by day
one after another
you will reach the last page

everyone likes
that version
quick, shortened, and edited

your life
is exciting
because it is limited

I tell you
the truth
take a deep breath

the best thing
about life
is actually death

coexist

struggling
to coexist
both lonely
and insane

ready to break
but not bend
fake pride and
real pain

women want more
men going their our own way
driving each other mad

relationships
are transaction
chivalry is dead

you are just a picture
pretentious fake
and lie

I'll also judge you
swiping
left or right

gratification is instant
harder
you may try

far apart already
isolated
further

accept, agree, accommodate
we complement
each other

poised

there was
a rabbit once
funny, fluffy, and fat

so full of himself
always bragging
about this and that

he used to
pick on a turtle
calling him slow and lazy

the turtle
was a chill out dude
felt the rabbit was crazy

the rabbit
dared the turtle
'let's have a race'

the turtle
knew that the results
will be obvious in this case

other animals
tried to push
and insist their choice

the turtle
heard everyone
but maintained his poise

he was
self-assured
and had no fear

after listening
to everyone
he made it clear

"I don't
need to prove anything
I can swim in the lakes"

"I count
on my strengths
not other's mistakes"

purpose

efforts
keep dreams
alive

all plans
no act
is naive

you can
relax
and wait for it

I have
a purpose
I can't sit

excuses
are
mind's lies

victory
is for the one
who tries

don't give up

stand by me
when no one
is around

don't give up
on us when
tough times hound

challenges come
demanding
our due

stick together
you love me and
I love you

it might seem
messed up
over and so done

weak divided
we are
stronger as one

original

I don't
get their jokes
I am fake laughing

the society
the formalities
it's a huge mocking

must I get married
celebrate events
birthdays, new year

things are odd
people are predictable
I'll die alone I fear

friends online
in real no one
is talking

am I awake
everyone is
sleepwalking

easy to blend in
original is what
I want to be

is there
something wrong
with me

now

dry as a desert
flourished
like forests

it keeps
changing seasons
life never rests

I never gave up
was always
determined

but time
is so precious
if more I could find

age is
not a number
it will wear you down

in the ocean
of time
you will finally drown

you will
be forgotten
just like the others

focus on
the present
if the future past bothers

in the midst
of this life
do your deeds well

for 'now' is here
be it
heaven or hell

why

starving
to fit
in those tiny pants

that model, that ad
perfect bodies
it all enchants

losing yourself
trying to look and sound
like that celebrity

your feet hurt
you still wear those shoes
how sad and pity

style, feel good
fashion, eat well
pamper yourself

be comfortable
be original
life will find itself

stop being critical
why so judgemental
this is self-cruelty

you are unique
stay true, stay original
let's redefine beauty

two people

when the passion
calms down
the reality sinks in

what's left
are two people
and 'lost love' between

build
the relationship
a little every day

there will be
ups and downs
you wish an easy way

watch
the finances
enrich mutual lives

no one else matters
with trust
your bond thrives

let go of small stuff
keep a
long term view

at the end
in lonely days
it's only both of you

the key

the key
is to know
when to let go

when the tide
is against
go with the flow

the root
of all misery is
the desire to control

with time
you'll realize
peace is the goal

you will
learn it eventually
but sooner is better

timing is important
for a mortal
it will matter

slowly
your mistakes
will accrue

finally
life will change
your view

a poem

like a river
a poem
flows

it has ups
and downs
highs and lows

It'll make
you think
and touch your heart

an escaped bird
an innocent laugh
a poem is a piece of art

my wish is not
to impress you or
impose my view

my hope is to
show a perspective
that is new

if you like my poems
smile, cry or
get an emotional hit

tell everyone
that
Charlie wrote it

journey

explore
the little pleasures
find happiness

let go of small stuff
be generous
with sorry and thanks

smile a bit
laugh a little
at least try

if not all
most will return
your 'hello' and 'hi'

it's a journey
we are on board
together

your memories
experiences, joy
are real treasure

don't know
who would check out
on the next station

enjoy the trip
we are headed to
the same destination

that one friend

a grave moment
but my friend seems
to be smirking

now I am distracted
I wonder
what is he thinking

he saw me
eyeing him and
busted out giggling

I had no clue
but I chuckled harder
rather then asking

embarrassed, stared at
trying to put
a serious face

just look at him
he is
a lost case

the black sheep
the free soul
life's celebration

long live that one friend
who laughs
at odd occasion

rituals

can't take my eyes off
I scanned you
from head to toe

look at you!
I want you now
won't take it slow

I could
just wait here
and hope for the best

keep desiring
and let destiny
do the rest

they say
there are
rules and rituals

follow them
feelings are less
important then visuals

this is not
how 'it' works and
society might disapprove

but this girl
is going to surprise you
and make the first move

not a bad guy

all I want is everything
the glitters and the bling
you criticize me, why?
I am not a bad guy

all I want is more for me
if some left give that to me
the bigger piece of pie
aiming the bullseye
ambitions are high
I am not a bad guy

it's not the greed
I have a higher need
wealth, worth and weed
I go and make it work
while you stand by
I am not a bad guy

I have seen poverty
I work you party
I am blunt, I am on a hunt
I don't sugar-coat, I don't lie
I am not a bad guy

yes, I want more
I have risen from the floor
the lessons I have learned
I demand, I have earned
I am hungry, I am sly
I am not a bad guy

my sweat, my possessions
don't get wrong impressions
I live the way I like
it's been a tough hike
before you judge me, stop!
it's lonely at the top
you'll know if you ever fly
I am not a bad guy

the bill

strange situation
here is an example
that is important

laying it out quietly
not at all going
on a rant

on a previous date
I suggested
to split the bill

traditional girl,
she promised to call
I am waiting still

this time
I went ahead
and paid it all

a feminist,
the look she gave
she'll never call

now every time
the check comes
I am scared

what do I do
the event is decisive
I feel dared

rather than
enjoying the moments
I am anxious

I am not being myself
neither is she
it's all pretentious

so pathetic
it tickles
my funny bone

you guessed it right
Charlie
will die alone

try

maybe
not now
but definitely later

for sure life
has planned
something better

the realities of life
are not
all glitter

there are things
you might not like
but they certainly matter

be kind
be positive
be humble

be persistent, be truthful
always get up
when you tumble

the truth is
as they say
'nobody gets out alive'

It's a journey
that will anyhow end
just go for a dive

give it your best shot
walk
if you can't fly

If you don't get it all
at least
you did try

I am you

I am you
from beginning
to beyond end

I am the witness
against me
you can't defend

you can hide
as much as
you want

put a mask
put a show
I see it, they can't

no matter what
nothing is hidden
from me

you can't
escape
run or flee

I'll chase you
show you the mirror
for I make you whole

scared?
look into my eyes
I am your soul

live

a few minutes
here
a few there

we waste time
our time
is so rare

complaining, hating
talking
behind backs

we waste
precious moments
each one stacks

think, feel
live, love
grab this opportunity

it'll be over soon
there is
no immunity

look closely
with every blink
of your eye

it's the life
your life
slipping by

a new day

a mug
full of coffee
I take a big gulp

what a beautiful morning
I could see
the sun coming up

nothing is in my control
not everything happens
the way I want

the future looks better
I'll reap tomorrow
today what I plant

a new day
few little things my way
and I am happy

It's not
too bad
I do feel lucky

© Charlie Windermere

Connect with Charlie Windermere

www.charliewindermere.com
www.facebook.com/charliewmere
www.instagram.com/charliewindermere
e-mail: author@charliewindermere.com

www.ingramcontent.com/pod-product-compliance
Lightning Source LLC
Chambersburg PA
CBHW020909080526
44589CB00011B/504